CHURCHES OF THE BANBURY AREA

St. Mary, Banbury

Churches of the Banbury Area

Drawings of the churches in the Deanery of Deddington and some others

by

GEORGE GRAHAM WALKER

With a Foreword by
RT. REV. D. G. LOVEDAY

KINETON · THE ROUNDWOOD PRESS · 1975

PUBLICATION OF THIS BOOK
HAS BEEN MADE POSSIBLE BY
ALCAN
A BANBURY CORPORATE RESIDENT
SINCE 1930

Set in 'Monotype' Bembo Series 270 12 on 14 pt, and printed by
Gordon Norwood at The Roundwood Press, Kineton
in the County of Warwick, England
and bound by Eric Neal, Welford, Rugby

Foreword

by the Rt. Rev. D. G. Loveday, formerly Bishop of Dorchester

THIS CHARMING BOOK is clearly the work of a talented artist, a thoughtful, perceptive, devout man. No introduction is necessary, though I am honoured to have been asked to write one: the author is well known locally and the book on examination makes an immediate appeal.

As Mr. Walker makes plain in his preface the book is primarily a collection of sketches to which a brief description of each church has been prefixed. But unlike books which illustrate the interior or some particular external feature of the buildings this collection of sketches reveals their exterior, and special attention has been paid to the setting of each church. In many of the drawings the juxtaposition of trees emphasises the unity between nature and man's creation. This is thoughtful and perceptive.

Just as parishes differ in character and in the outlook and temperament of the inhabitants, so each church leaves its particular impression on the visitor – sometimes, as in the description of Mollington, this devout Churchman has been impressed by the manifest loving care of the worshippers in preparation for a festival as well as by their work of restoration.

I have known every one of these churches for well over half a century and have ministered and worshipped in them all. I am confident that this book will be greatly valued and will help to bring home to all who see it the greatness of the heritage which is ours and our duty as trustees of that inheritance to maintain and hand on to future generations these churches to be honoured, loved and used.

✠ D. G. LOVEDAY

FOR MY WIFE

Companion in my travels

Contents

Pages on which drawings appear are given in bold type

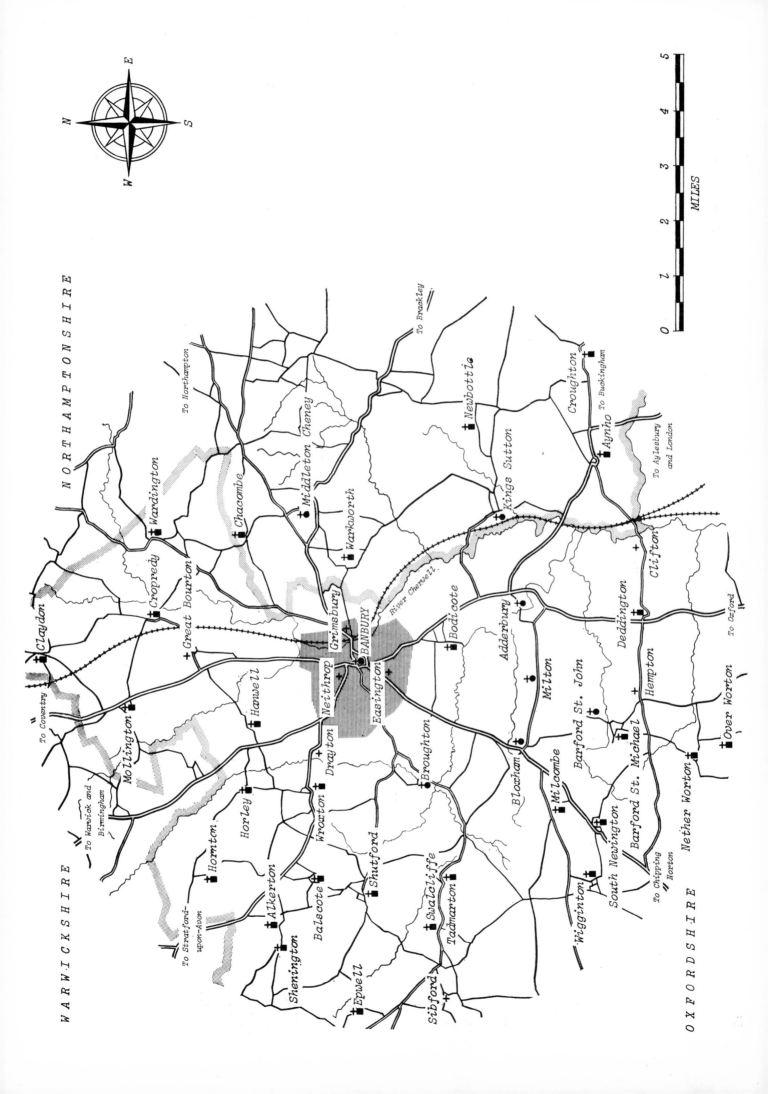

Introduction

WILLIAM WORDSWORTH celebrated his visit to North Oxfordshire with a sonnet 'A Parsonage in Oxfordshire'. It was written while staying with the rector of Souldern and gives a brief word picture of the parsonage, church and churchyard.

Born within six miles of Wordsworth's birthplace a century and a half later, I have no ability to express in the same way as the greatest of all fellow-Cumbrians the affection I feel for the part of Oxfordshire that has been my home for the past twenty-five years. Cumberland (or Cumbria, as we must now call it) is surely God's own county – or why would it be blessed with the loveliest scenery?– but North Oxfordshire has its own serene beauty and in this attractive landscape its churches stand out as pure gold. Different in materials, in setting, and often in character, from those in the Lake Counties, they nevertheless enslaved me on sight and it was as natural for me to express this enchantment in drawing (whatever its shortcomings) as it was for Wordsworth to express his in verse.

Living within the Deanery of Deddington, and in a very small way being actively engaged in it, I was driven to draw every one of its churches, and these form the basis of this book. Architecturally and historically some of the churches could no doubt be omitted. They are included because every church, whatever its character is held in affection by somebody: those who regularly use it, those who were baptised, confirmed or married in it, those who live near it, and those who simply like it to be there. Moreover, this area, like every other, is for economic reasons faced with church closures and it is the less architecturally and historically interesting that will disappear.

So this is essentially a book of drawings. The words will, I hope add to their interest: they can do little more, for space is limited and I claim to be an enthusiast, not an expert. Anyone requiring fuller information must look elsewhere, for example in the Victoria History and the Oxfordshire and Northamptonshire volumes in the Penguin Buildings of England series by Nikolaus Pevsner, each a masterpiece of its kind, and in local guidebooks, while those requiring an architectural assessment will also consult John Betjeman's 'Collins Pocket Guide to English Parish Churches'.

I gratefully acknowledge the assistance of these and various books mentioned in the text, notably Bdly Beesley's 'History of Banbury'. I am indebted also to the clergy. I share with them, in some degree, the privilege which is beyond price, of being licensed to conduct services in these churches. And worshipping in them is the best way of knowing them.

I am especially grateful to Bishop Loveday for his most generous introduction and for numerous suggestions which have improved the text. His unequalled knowledge of, and love for, the churches of the Banbury area in which he has long ministered, and with many of which his family is historically linked, is well known.

Finally, I must express my gratitude to Alcan, my employer for quarter of a century, without whose support this book would not have been published.

Bodicote

G. G. W.

1

St Mary, Adderbury

ADDERBURY

ONE SHOULD HAVE been prepared for the church by the splendour of Adderbury's fine houses, notably the gabled seventeenth century house by the Green where William III's minister, Lord Montague, lived and Adderbury House of later date once the home of the poet John Wilmot, Earl of Rochester, and afterwards of the second Duke of Argyll who entertained Alexander Pope.

One should have been prepared also by the famous spire and the magnificent Decorated exterior with its great windows. Nevertheless the first glimpse of the church interior was breathtaking. The magic was worked by the proportions, as in an instant one was transported from a village to a cathedral city. Leisurely examination picked out the elements that contributed to the effect and did not find the extensive restoration work of Sir Gilbert Scott objectionable.

The church's focal point, its chancel, was built in Perpendicular style early in the 15th century by Richard of Winchcombe for William of Wykeham, whose armorial bearings and bust may be seen carved in the chancel roof and in its outside wall. The east wall is richly adorned with sculptured figures of later date including lifesized figures of the Virgin and the Angel Gabriel at each side of the window and smaller figures of the Apostles forming the reredos. The chancel has numerous interesting features, from the grave of the vicar shot by Roundhead soldiers in the Civil War to the grotesque figures carved under the seats of the choir stalls. The chancel arch frames a fine 15th century screen, and on the wall above it are traces of paintings.

The nave arcades and the transepts are of the 13th century, and the capitals of two pillars supporting the arches between aisles and transepts command special attention being decorated with heads and figures.

Apart from its architectural features, the body of the church is full of interest: for example, two brasses of 1460 and 1508 are favourites for rubbing; there is an oak chest of 1725 with ironwork three hundred years older; and there is a painted memorial of 1586 with the kneeling figures of one Thomas More and his wife.

No visitor to Adderbury Church, even someone lacking the Faith that built it, could ever feel alone. Carved faces and figures gaze and grimace from many places both inside the church and outside. Round the sturdy 13th century tower surmounted by its equally sturdy spire, meriting its place in the rhyme

Bloxham for length,
Adderbury for strength
Kings Sutton for beauty,

is a fantastic gallery of humans, musicians and mermaids, birds and animals, natural and grotesque, laughable and frightening, continuing along the cornices of both aisles. They seem to make all the more exquisite the tracery of the windows (which was removed in 1788 from those in the body of the church to let in more light and later replaced) and the beauty of the vestry's semi-oriel window.

The tower offers a very fine view in which the spires of Bloxham and Kings Sutton are landmarks. It also gives sight of the aluminium roof (using metal produced at the Banbury works) which was more than paid for by the sale of the perished lead, producing a successful marriage of the 13th century and the 20th.

Dragon at Adderbury

ALKERTON

ALKERTON CHURCH STANDS high on a hill, almost hidden by trees, and after climbing up to it by way of the steep winding steps from the village below you may imagine that the time-worn figures facing you from the cornice under the 14th century south aisle parapet are mocking your breathlessness. An attractive building, especially when its golden stone glows in the sun and is

Beside the south wall of the chancel is the worn effigy of an unknown knight in armour of the 13th century, but of Alkerton's most famous son, Thomas Lydyat, buried in the chancel, there is no memorial, not even the remains of the simple inscription incised by New College stating that he was 'the faithful pastor of that church'. Yet he has a memorial in print, in the lines Samuel Johnson wrote on The Vanity of Human Wishes:

There mark what ills the scholar's life assail,
Toil, envy, want, the patron and the jail,
See nations, slowly wise, and meanly just,
To buried merit raise the tardy bust.
If dreams yet flatter, once again attend,
Hear Lydyat's life, and Galileo's end.

Lydyat certainly knew misfortune – and jail. Born here in 1572, son of the lord of the manor, he was baptised in the 12th century font we now see. Winning a European reputation as a scholar through his writings on history, astronomy and 'chronography' he became chaplain at the court of James I and tutor to Henry, Prince of Wales. The prince died young, and with him Lydyat's hope of preferment, and after a short time in Ireland he returned to Alkerton in 1612 as rector. He continued to write, but having pledged himself as security for a friend, found himself in debt and was imprisoned in the jails of Oxford, Warwick and Banbury. He died poor in 1646.

However, there *is* a memorial to Lydyat in stone – the very fine Jacobean rectory he built in 1625, just a short step from the church that saw his beginning and his end.

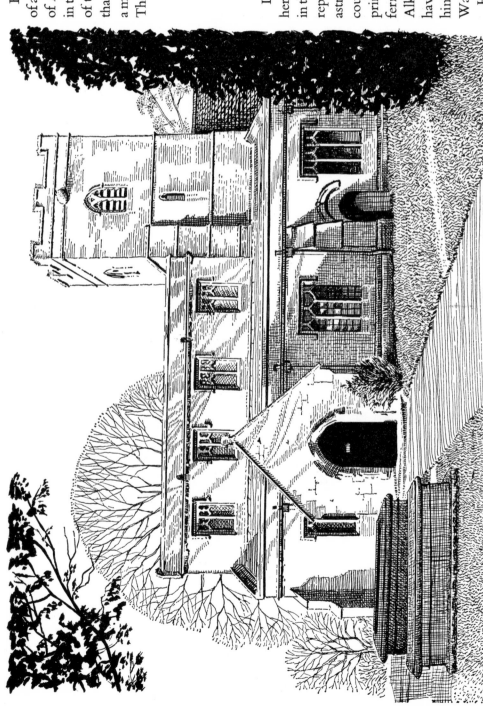

St Michael, Alkerton

patterned by the shadows of the bare trees, it is, as its present rector writes 'noble yet homely, solid but not oppressive'. Certainly, the central tower, dating from the 12th century with additions from the 14th, accentuates its solidity, and inside the church is small and intimate with a south aisle which shares the ground plan with a nave and chancel is barely six feet wide and, as the rector points out, the square-headed windows are more usual in a house than a church.

A key to its nobility is the fine 13th century tower arch, through which the simple raised chancel is seen, and the wide bays of the south arcade of the same period, while the whole interior is well lit by nave, aisle and clerestory windows of a century later.

BALSCOTE

SHARING ONE OF the hills on which the village is built, the church overlooks houses of local stone and thatch and the village green down in a hollow on the outskirts. The church is seen best in south elevation, from the farm-

4

St. Mary Magdalene, Balscote

Entrance is through the very small south porch form-

ing the base of the church's most distinctive feature, a slim
tower made graceful by standing away from the nave and
clerestory by the width of the south aisle. The church is
largely of the Decorated period from which the tower

also dates except for its elegantly pinnacled upper storey
which was added in the 15th century.

Four Decorated arches separate the single, south, aisle
from the nave, two of the pillars showing carved heads

among trees half-way up the hill.

house opposite, but is entered by way of a wicket gate

framed in head-dresses of the period. The Decorated windows give the church much of its character, especially those in the chancel, the east window with its elaborate tracery being particularly fine. The 14th century is recalled also by the two piscinae, in the chancel and south aisle.

The present building replaced a Norman church, from which has come the tub font, its lead lining overlapping the rim in a pattern, and a small roundheaded doorway, now blocked up, in the north wall of the nave and thought to be part of a tympanum.

A surprising feature is the elaborate carving on the pulpit, literally foreign in this setting. A gift of Col. North, Wroxton Abbey, it is the work of a continental woodcarver of three or four centuries ago – a European import, like the Norman genius that set the style of the first church on this spot.

BANBURY

THE PRESENT PARISH church of Banbury will always suffer from the reputation of its predecessor. Without exception, every printed reference to the 'old' church pays tribute to its magnificence, usually with the phrase 'worthy to have been a cathedral', and this description is confirmed by contemporary drawings. But a very common tendency to belittle the present church is encouraged as much by the manner of the old church's end as by its character. To say that it was pulled down in 1790, being considered too costly to repair, is to understate the case. Despite its shaky condition it did not come down easily, and to read the details of its remains is to experience a unique horror. As is often said, the destruction of Banbury's 'cathedral' is only one episode – though the chief – in a history of destruction, which has included its

St. Mary, Banbury

Cross, its castle and more recently its cake shop, and perhaps to these could be added the destruction of much of its character by some graceless new building.

The old church was a Gothic edifice, largely a product of the 14th and 15th centuries but with much of the nave and aisles of the two centuries before. Its tower was plain Perpendicular with eight pinnacles, (as seen now in Deddington). The present church could hardly be more different. It is in late classical style, comprising a large square nave on three sides of which are spacious galleries, the fourth opening into the chancel with an apsidal sanctuary. The great central dome, the roof and the galleries are supported by twelve Ionic columns. At the west end is the familiar columned portico over which rises the distinctive circular tower, the popular name for which – 'the pepper pot' – aptly describes its shape. Built of Hornton stone, the church rises somewhat phoenix-like from the stone of the old church in its foundations, apart from which only the organ, an oil painting of the Virgin with the dead Christ, and the 14th century font now in the churchyard have survived.

The main body of the new church was opened for worship in 1797, but owing to expense the portico and tower were not completed until 1822. Hence the couplet

Dirty Banbury's proud people
Built a Church without a steeple

It should be explained that Banbury was 'dirty' largely because of the soft loamy soil producing excessively muddy streets after rain.

The interior as it is seen today is not as it was when first built. A fourth gallery extended across the east wall masking the upper part of the chancel, which had a lower roof and no apse. The east wall had two windows at each side above the gallery level, with the organ centrally placed between them, and the oil painting of the pieta

St. Hugh, Easington

Banbury Cross

reigns Christ in Glory and the chancel ceiling is bright blue with gold stars. Pale blue is a predominant colour in the nave and there is a gilded text round the dome. The windows of Victorian glass are rich in detail, the upper row depicting scenes from the life of Christ, and the lower some of the parables.

Refurbishing in 1960 displayed the interior in all its glory and won the reluctant admiration of some who had not known what to make of the strange interior, while others found it vulgar; but to those who loved the church – and there are many – it seemed to acquire a new life.

Demolition was the fate of another Banbury church in more recent times – the church of South Banbury. To make better provision for the growing population, especially the poor who found the pew rents of St. Mary's prohibitive, this new parish was created in 1846 and Christ Church (architect, Benjamin Ferrey) was built to serve it in 1853. Increase of population in the Grimsbury area created a similar problem, which was resolved by building the Church of St. Leonard, *Grimsbury* as a chapel of ease to the parish of South Banbury in 1890. In 1921 Grimsbury was constituted as a separate parish. This had repercussions over forty years later when South Banbury, much reduced in size by the secession of Grimsbury, was again greatly reduced by the movement of population from the town centre to new estates on the outskirts. As a result, South Banbury was reunited with Banbury in 1967 and Christ Church was closed and demolished.

Both Christ Church and St. Leonard's were built in the spirit of the Oxford Movement and it is ironic that the Grimsbury church, once the daughter church and much less impressive, still flourishes. Comprising nave, two aisles and chancel, with south porch and bell turret, its furnishings bespeak its tradition. The roof members are supported by figures of angels holding crests bearing

St. Leonard, Grimsbury

formed the altar-piece. Standing out from the south pillar supporting this gallery was a three-tier pulpit. When the east gallery was removed in 1858 the organ was divided and placed on either side of the chancel, to be moved again to its present chamber on the north side in

1873, the year the chancel was heightened and the apse formed. Three years later the interior decoration, under Sir Arthur Blomfield, was complete, but not exactly as we see it today in all its gilt and brilliant colours. Round the walls of the apse are the twelve Apostles; above them symbols of the Passion, and a rood hangs in the chancel arch, with figures of Our Lady and St. John the Divine on either side. A lady chapel was added in 1926 and furnished with a memorial window depicting Our Lady in Glory. The reredos largely covering the east window was erected as a memorial in 1950, while the rondels depicting the Stations of the Cross, which were formerly in Christ Church, commemorate the relationship between the two churches.

Two further Anglican churches were opened in Banbury for the convenience of worshippers living at some distance from St. Mary's. In 1853, the year Christ Church was built, St. Paul's was opened as a chapel of ease at *Neithrop* to the north. It is Early English in style, consisting of nave, north aisle, chancel and south porch, its main entrance being at the west end opening on to the main Warwick Road. To serve the new estate at *Easington*, in the south, St. Hugh's was opened in 1933. This is a dual purpose building combining the functions of church and church hall, with one end, containing an altar, serving as a sanctuary that can be closed off as required.

The planned expansion of the town's population to 40,000 raises continuous problems for the Church as for other authorities. Tourists to this town made world famous through the nursery rhyme are unaware of such difficulties as they photograph the substitute 19th century Cross with St. Mary's in the background, and then move closer to photograph the church itself, with the Tudor vicarage beside it an exquisite reminder of Banbury's more distant past.

Jonathan Swift is said to have lodged in a house on the opposite side of the Horse Fair and to have taken the name Gulliver for the hero of his most famous book from a tombstone in the churchyard. Part of the house next door to the vicarage was once an 18th century inn kept by one, Samuel Gulliver.

St. Paul, Neithrop

ing nave and chancel only. With very extensive restoration during the 19th century, including the erection of an octagonal shingle spire over the south porch, it also less obviously shows its ancient origin. Largely concealed by a fine manor house to the west and a farmyard to the south, the way into the churchyard is not easy to find. Through the porch the doorway into the nave is plain Norman, with four rows of chevron moulding. The font is of the same period, while the chancel arch and chancel with its double-lancet window in the south wall is Early English. The niche for a piscina in the south-east corner of the chancel is probably later. The south wall and windows remain from 14th century rebuilding in the Decorated style, together with Perpendicular windows from the 15th century. These were all retained in the extensive restoration of last century, when the present tower was erected to replace one in mediaeval style that rose from the south-west corner of the nave.

A half-mile walk across the bridge brings one to the church of Great Barford or *Barford St. Michael* much more conspicuously placed on high ground and with a tower that emphasises its age. Squat and thick-walled, the tower is Norman, like both doorways, but it is the north doorway, high, fairly narrow and richly decorated, that leaves the strongest impression. It is an Iffley of North Oxon, with its wealth of beak-heads and chevron ornament covering arch and columns and finely carved knot-work in the tympanum. The tub font is also Norman.

Much of the remainder of the fabric is of the 14th century. The high, well-lit nave is separated by two pillars from the single, south, aisle, at the east end of which the tower stands. The chancel arch has carved capitals, probably from an earlier period, and is fitted with a 15th century carved and painted screen. The woodwork of the pulpit was carved some two or three hundred

Barford St. John

THE BARFORDS

A VERY SHORT step apart, on either side of the River Swere meandering among willows, these twin hamlets make a strong appeal to country-lovers looking for a home. Recently some new building has enlarged both communities, but they are still so small – and so close together – that their separate churches may appear a

luxury. For years they have had no resident parson, and rationalisation due to manpower shortage could at some future date curtail regular worship in either. Yet, very different in character, both are much loved and their continuing life is much to be desired.

Formerly a chapel under Adderbury, the church of Little Barford, or *Barford St. John*, is the smaller, compris-

years later, but it is thought that the hexagonal stone base is from an older stone pulpit.

A tall lancet window in the somewhat forbidding west wall contrasts with the Decorated windows of the nave and aisle and the east window with its depressed arch. One of the windows contains three diamond-shaped panes bearing a crowned 'H' of Saxon form in yellow. In the floor near the chancel are two brasses with portraits of Sir William Fox and his wife. At the west end of the south aisle hangs an interesting drawing of the Last Judgment.

Not far from the church is the vicarage, of the same stone as the church, dating from the 17th century but largely rebuilt.

BLOXHAM

IT IS THE spire of Bloxham Church that is most widely known – 'Bloxham for length' – and certainly it pinpoints the village for many miles around. But its length is matched by its beauty, although the rhyme reserves that quality for Kings Sutton. Tower and spire together, soaring to 198 feet, merit a book of their own, as a splendid integration of square and octagonal forms, of buttresses and pinnacles, windows and ornament: a 14th century monument of ascending grace. But the tower is the lure to other, equal, enchantments not least the magnificent windows, Decorated and Perpendicular, which one admires outside for their shape and their tracery and then all over again for their glass; and the extravagant decoration, from the carvings of the great west doorway representing the Apostles, the Passion and the Day of Judgment, to the comical parade of men and animals on the cornice of the north aisle.

The church is entered by the Early English south porch which has a priest's room above it and incorporates stone-

Barford St. Michael

work from an earlier Norman church. Other portions of this church are to be seen in the Early English chancel, namely the columns and capitals of the chancel arch, the richly ornamented arches of the south windows (including beak-heads) and the doorway into the vestry. Here also,

in contrast, is one of the church's later additions, the east window by William Morris and Edward Burne-Jones. The chancel screen was restored in 1866 but retains much of the 15th century, including painted panels in red and gold.

The nave arcades are Early English, like the chancel, but the aisle on each side and the north transept are of the 14th century like the tower and spire. The great Perpendicular windows of the south aisle and the south transept known as the Milcombe Chapel are of a century later. The north transept has a particularly fine clustered column with a capital beautifully carved with knights' heads and linked arms – appropriate to what is now called the War Memorial Chapel.

Bloxham is not popularly associated with wall paintings, but there are the remains of a Doom over the chancel arch and of a St. Christopher over the north door, both from the 14th century. There are later paintings between the windows of the Milcombe Chapel, but these are overshadowed by the ornate 18th century tomb of Sir John Thornycroft, 'Baronett of Milcomb,' an elegantly reclining figure with hand upraised.

On the wall of the north aisle are three appealing 18th century brasses, but the glory of this aisle is the Decorated west window with its very attractive tracery carved with the head of Christ and symbols of the four evangelists.

Among much other stone carving, which makes the church as richly ornamented inside as outside, is a variety of figures beneath the roof, and, far below, the 14th century font with each of its eight panels carved to represent a Decorated window separated by pinnacled buttresses. It is a font splendidly appropriate to its setting. The architect responsible for the 19th century restoration, G. E. Street, also designed Bloxham School which dominates the other end of the village.

BODICOTE

IN BODICOTE THE Church is represented not by one building but by several, identified by the diocesan arms

St. Mary, Bloxham

12

St. John the Baptist, Bodicote

or the cross of St. John the Baptist. On entering the village from Banbury over a flyover that has partly covered the 'rhubarb field' where the plant was once grown for medicinal purposes to provide a small village industry, one passes first the vicarage, then the church school (its building financed largely by parishioners), before coming to the church itself. It is flanked by the church house on one side and its youth centre (formerly the school) on the other. A few yards away stand a court

of old people's flats and their common room erected and managed by the church housing association.

There has been a church here since the 13th century, originally as a chapel-of-ease to Adderbury, but from that building only the chancel arch, with its moulded capitals and the tub font (rescued from a farmyard and reinstated in 1918) remain.

The church was rebuilt in the 14th century with the addition of north and south aisles, and the simple arched

nave arcades date from this period. In the 15th century a tower was added, rising from the middle of the north aisle, but was demolished and replaced by the present tower at the west end when the church was almost completely rebuilt and enlarged in 1843-4. During these extensive alterations, the mediaeval rood loft was re-moved, and a singers' gallery erected in 1766 was replaced by an organ at the west end. During further work in 1878 the organ was moved to its present position in the chancel,

13

the vestry became the organ chamber and a new vestry was made at the foot of the tower.

The east window, with its stained glass installed in 1847 has provoked controversy, both aesthetic and theological, having the Saviour on the same level as St. John the Baptist (the patron saint), St. Peter and St. Paul. It has rich glowing colours and is much more impressive than the other memorial windows nevertheless. The stone memorials on the interior walls include one to James Barnes, who was chief engineer for the Grand Trunk Canal linking the Trent with the Mersey. A famous scholar, baptised here on 23rd November 1616 no doubt in the same tub font, was John Kersey, author of 'The Elements of Mathematical Art commonly called Algebra' and friend of Edmund Wingate whose book on arithmetic he revised in several editions. He did not stay long in Bodicote, however: his fame as a teacher of mathematics was earned in London.

The village is proud of the church's turret clock (dated 1701) which was renovated in 1973 by the parish council, through public subscription.

BROUGHTON

THERE CAN BE few churches of its size giving such an immediate welcome into history. Certainly, one is prepared for this by the castle, so close that the moat bounds the churchyard. The Elizabethan north front is seen as one approaches through the elmed park and is glimpsed through the 15th century gateway tower as one opens the churchyard gate. The castle has been described in Pevsner as 'the most complete mediaeval house in the county'. Parts of it were built in the 14th century, including its own tiny chapel, and it is from the same period that the church itself dates, although the Norman font and the mid-13th century arcade are evidence of an earlier church, and there have been later additions, including the 15th century clerestory.

The historical link is more strongly forged, however, by the castle being the home (open on certain days to visitors) of Lord Saye and Sele, the descendant of the church soldiers, statesmen and divines whom the church commemorates in its fabric, its tombs and memorials over six centuries.

The most striking monument is the earliest, that of the builder of the church and castle, Sir John de Broughton who died in 1315. He lies in effigy, under a richly coloured canopy, in the wall of the church's one, south, aisle, but somewhat overshadowed by a 16th century tomb intended for Edward Fiennes, one of the family which has owned the castle since 1451. Crowding the east end of the aisle, there are also an attractive 15th century brass, a decorated 13th century stone coffin lid and a composite tomb surmounted by an effigy.

In the chancel are two other tombs: one of William Fiennes, the first Lord Saye and Sele (prominent in the Civil War and Lord Privy Seal after the Restoration, when he acquired the nickname 'Old Subtlety' for his astuteness) and his wife; the other a double-effigied tomb of Sir Thomas and Lady Wykeham, the great niece of William of Wykeham, Chancellor of England in 1388 and also Bishop of Winchester who acquired the castle from the de Broughtons. Dim remnants of wall paintings and an imposing array of hatchments look down on these tombs and the graves of four other Viscounts Saye and Sele buried in the chancel. It is easy to overlook a rare Crucifixion painted on the pillar behind the font, thought to represent the Blood of Life flowing into the Water of Baptism.

Of all the carved stonework in the church, including the beautiful tracery of the windows, both Decorated and Perpendicular, the most precious is the 14th century rood screen, a rarity in stone and as intricately carved as if it were timber.

The attractive variety of windows and doorways enhances the appeal of the church's exterior, the whole crowned by a good early Decorated tower, its broach spire relieved by gabled windows. This is the last one sees of the church through the old elms on leaving the park.

Broughton Castle

St. Mary the Virgin, Broughton

St. James, Claydon

16

CLAYDON

LEAVING THE MAIN Banbury to Coventry road, and setting your face and your step towards Claydon in rural isolation on top of its 'clay hill', you could imagine it lost, miles from anywhere. But it is pin-pointed on the map half-a-mile from the Three Shires Stone as the northernmost outpost of Oxfordshire.

It is a small village, encircling a small church which is distinguished in this part of the county for the saddleback roof on its small time-worn 14th century tower. Spanning eight or nine centuries, the church, of local stone, was extensively restored in 1860, the work according to Bishop Wilberforce (who preached at its reopening) being 'very nicely done and the church very pretty'. The round-headed south porch, its door bearing the date 1640 leads into the nave and beyond it an extremely narrow north aisle, separated by a 12th century arcade of four bays. The chancel is a continuation of the nave, and from it a doorway leads into a very attractive tiny chapel added to the east end of the north aisle in the 13th century. This is perhaps a chantry chapel, rarely found in such a small church as this. It has been suggested that since the stones on the chancel side of the small door are weathered, this was the outer door to the chapel before the chancel was built. A curious external feature is the pointed medieval chimney stack above the north aisle.

From the tower the hours ring out from a clock thought to have been made locally in the 17th century and modified a century later. It has since been repaired but parishioners have to be satisfied with being told the time by the hour, for the clock has no face.

Within the first century of Claydon church, in the reign of King John, a priory was founded at Clattercote, about a mile to the south. Remains of it are to be seen in the farmhouse there, notably in a vaulted and groined chamber and in a dovecote.

St. James, Clifton

CLIFTON

LIKE STONES IN a necklace, the hamlets of Clifton and Hampton are strung on the same road a mile and a half equidistant from Deddington with which they have always been inseparably linked. Or, to change the simile, Deddington has always taken the two hamlets under her wings, and this is especially true in matters ecclesiastical.

17

St. Mary the Virgin, Cropredy

All three are more popularly linked in rhyme:

Aynho on the hill,
Clifton on the clay,
Dirty, drunken, Deddington,
And Hempton high way.

Down a hill from both Deddington and Aynho, Clifton reclines in the valley of the Cherwell. Its name is recorded over at least eight centuries, but the present church gives no evidence of history or of its predecessor. As H. M. Colvin notes in his 'History of Deddington', the existence of an earlier church is recorded only at Somerset House, in a sixteenth century bequest of 6s 8d to 'Clifton Chapell' but of the site there is no sign.

The church that now stands on the north side of the Aynho-Deddington road owes its existence largely to the initiative and generosity of a former Vicar of Deddington, Rev. W. C. Risley, who laid the foundation stone in 1851, three years after resigning the living. Built in the Early English style, the church comprises simply a continuous nave and chancel, with a south porch and a bell-cote at the west end. It was consecrated in 1853, and its recent closure – exactly 120 years later – is a sign of these times of smaller congregations, greater mobility and limited manpower. So Clifton's churchpeople now worship at Deddington again.

CROPREDY

IT IS in the church and churchyard that one finds the most vivid reminders of Cropredy's place in history. For not far away, on the edge of the village, stands Cropredy Bridge round which was fought the famous early battle of the Civil War on 29th June 1644, when the Royalists led by Charles I in person won a victory over the Parliamentarians under General Waller.

In the churchyard can be seen gravestones commemorating soldiers who died that day, and in the church itself displayed suits of armour, helmets and cannon balls. Examine the magnificent brass eagle lectern and you find a further reminder of the battle in the shape of a bronze lion. Serving as one of the feet, it does not exactly match the other two. It appears that the villagers hid their lectern in the River Cherwell rather than see it desecrated by Waller's troops and when it was recovered about fifty years later it was minus one of the lions, which was eventually made good by a local craftsman. A guidebook compiled by Cropredy schoolchildren a few years ago quotes from the churchwardens' accounts: '1695. Paid Dame White for scouring the eagle, 2d', presumably when the lectern was reinstated.

Parts of the church ante-date the Battle of Cropredy by four centuries. The nave and south aisle show traces of 13th century work, and the octagonal font (which stood in the vicarage garden for a number of years) and the parish chest (which is said to have been loaded with the church plate and thrown into the river with the lectern) are of the same period. In the 14th century the lofty nave arcades were built, the arches of which are specially graceful with Decorated mouldings rising in a continuous line from the base, (only paralleled locally at Ratley) and the clerestory was erected adding height and light to the nave. During the same period the chancel was built, with a tall arch matching those in the nave and with the fine east window. The tower, which has a similar arch at the west end of the nave, and the south porch are also of the 14th century.

Decorated windows; the north aisle was altered and given fine Decorated windows; the south aisle with its Perpendicular windows is of later date, and the chapels were added later by extending the aisles along the sides of the chancel. There are two piscinae: a double one, decorated with trefoiled openings, in the chancel, and another, perpendicular, in the north aisle.

The screens in the south chapel contain mediaeval woodwork and the carved pulpit has been dated 1619. One of the north aisle windows contains a fragment of old glass. There are numerous memorials, including memorial windows, and also the sketchy remains of wall paintings, including a Doom over the chancel arch.

Obviously, restoration over the years has modified the work of previous centuries, but the total effect of the church today is of a spacious building predominantly 14th century, of great beauty and much dignity.

Cropredy's lectern

SS Peter and Paul, Deddington

DEDDINGTON

ONE'S FIRST IMPRESSION of the church tower, large in area and massive in structure, utterly dwarfing every building in the square, is that is will never fall down. The first one did, in 1634, bringing down much of the Church with it, so the rebuilders evidently took heed.

Deddington was once much more important that it is now. Built on a hill, commanding a valley on each side and standing at an important crossroads, the town had a castle (now only a grassy mound) and fine houses of which the most impressive survivor is Castle House. This mansion originated in the 13th century, but the familiar three-storied gabled and balustraded building is of the 17th century. Situated just north of the church, Castle House was formerly the rectory. Here Piers Gaveston was lodged in 1312, whence he was taken for execution on Blacklow Hill, and here Charles I slept before the Battle of Cropredy Bridge in 1644. Charles saw the church bells that had fallen down with the tower and he had them melted down for cannon balls.

As the parish church of an important town, the church of SS Peter and Paul was built on a large scale. Both aisles are unusually wide (almost as wide as the nave) which could mean that the original 12th century church was cruciform. No trace of this church remains. The fine windows identify the present building as a mixture of Decorated and Perpendicular, but while the 14th and 15th centuries predominate there is much work from the 13th – the chancel, for example, including the stonework of the windows and the sedilia and piscina.

The chancel screen, however, was erected in the 15th century and, though much restored, retains some of its original tracery. The 13th century building of the nave and aisles, still evidenced by the north and south doorways, is masked by 14th century rebuilding, including the nave arcades which retain three of the old columns, and some of the windows.

In the 15th century, both nave and chancel were transformed by the addition of the clerestory, and the south aisle by the inclusion of the handsome window of five lights in the south wall. The fine Perpendicular windows in the east wall of both aisles are probably of a century later. During considerable restoration work in the last century, the present vestry and south porch were built, and the interior walls of the church were stripped of their plaster, as we now see them. This restoration was undertaken by G. E. Street who was responsible for the impressive east window depicting the Crucifixion, with the Last Supper and Resurrection.

The church has no elaborate monuments and some of the memorials that are here have been abused. The oldest monument, of the 14th century, is an effigy of a lawyer in a recess in the south wall. In the north aisle, the altar tomb of William Billing (died 1533) has been mutilated by the removal of the metal figures of him and his wife. Part of a brass showing a man of the reign of Edward III is fixed to a column of the north arcade.

There are numerous wall tablets, but perhaps the most striking memorial of all is a group of nine wooden crosses from Flanders commemorating Deddington men who died in the 1914-18 war. 'The parish that remembers' was how Arthur Mee described the present writer's home parish of Clifton, Cumbria which similarly brought back the crosses of its war dead and lined the path up to the church with them. The same could be said of Deddington.

DRAYTON

NORTH OXFORDSHIRE ABOUNDS in churches that dominate their villages from a hilltop. Drayton church, on the other hand, is virtually hidden at the edge of the village. Quietly situated in a deep hollow, almost encircled by meadowland, it has to be searched out, and the tower is no guide, for it rises little higher than the roof of the nave. This adds to the simple and unostentatious exterior of the building and matches the simplicity of worship firmly associated with this church over two centuries led by a succession of rectors in the Evangelical tradition.

In fact, however, the tower, which was entirely rebuilt in 1808, would have been surmounted by a spire if plans drawn up in 1877 for the extensive repair and alteration of the church had been fully implemented.

In Drayton, as in so many other churches, the font is the oldest feature, the one relic of the original building. The fount of Christian initiation in perpetual use through centuries of change, it represents the continuous life of the Church militant. Drayton's font is Norman, plain with carved ropework at the rim, while the fabric of the church is mainly of the 14th century, much restored a hundred years ago.

The 14th century arcades that separate the nave from the two aisles have three arches surmounted by a clerestory of the last century. The capital of one of the nave pillars is carved with busts of three knights with arms interlaced and, to keep them company, corbel heads look down from the roof. Three heads also look out from the arches over two Decorated sedilia, alongside a piscina, unusually placed in the south aisle.

Several tombs commemorate known and unknown knights, clergy and humble parishioners. The oldest tomb, a stone coffin of the 13th century, occupies a recess in the north wall. Its lid carved with foliage gives no sign whose body it contained, but it is thought to have been that of the church's founder. At the east end of the south aisle curtained off as a vestry is the altar tomb of William Greville who died in 1440 and whose likeness is engraved

St. Peter, Drayton

22

on the lid. He was the eldest son of Ludovic Greville who died two years earlier and once occupied with his wife Margaret a tomb on the north side of the chancel. The alabaster slab from this tomb, incised with their figures (now partly obliterated) is in the floor of the belfry.

Among several rectors who are commemorated, one from the 18th century, Rev. John Dover, speaks from the grave through the inscription on a tablet in the chancel wall:

Lo, here your late unworthy rector lies,
Who, though he's dead, loud as he can, replies,
Repent . . .

But his call doesn't disturb the peace of this secluded spot.

EPWELL

'IN THE GENERAL appearance of this village, which is very peculiar, there is something primitive, and which not only pervades the character of its inhabitants, but also their various habitations. Even the church itself, being unadorned, and devoid of any pretensions to architectural beauty, is not exempt from this simplicity of style'. Much has happened since Skelton wrote that in 1823 to make the inhabitants and their habitations less primitive, while modern taste finds architectural beauty in the unadorned simplicity of Epwell Church. However, here in the shadow of Epwell Hill there are still views to satisfy anybody with a taste for the picturesque, in which the simplicity of thatched cottages has a part.

The church is like that of Balscote on the other side of the valley of Sor Brook in having its tower over the south porch, although Epwell's robust embattled tower could hardly be more different from Balscote's. Epwell is unusual in that the tower, with its porch, forms the west end of the south aisle, opening on to the nave reading desk.

St. Anne, Epwell

through two arches. The structure of this small church is largely of the 13th century with alterations in the 14th, including heightening of the tower and building of new windows and a piscina in the chancel. The octagonal font may also date from the 14th century. The pulpit is from the 17th and Jacobean work can be identified also in the reading desk.

Work on the chancel has been recorded in the 15th and 17th centuries, and it still retains its lead roof installed exactly two hundred years ago. The whole church underwent major restoration in the middle of last century when it was in a very bad state of repair, and from these modifications, including removal of a singers' gallery, an appealingly simple, uncluttered interior has emerged.

GREAT BOURTON

ON TURNING OFF the main road, one's first impression of the distant bell tower-cum-lych gate is that it is the gateway to the village. Closer inspection shows that it does dominate both the main road and the church, while from their hilltop the church and bell tower together command a broad view over Great Bourton, Cropredy and the Cherwell valley.

The gateway with its bell tower was erected in 1882, some years after the church was restored and brought into use for the first time since the Reformation. Built in the early 14th century, the church was desecrated in the 16th, and writing in 1841 Beesley said the chancel was all that remained of the church in a tolerable state. It was being used as a schoolroom, the chancel arch was walled up, and the nave used as a schoolhouse and a grocer's shop. With their own church closed to worship, parishioners from Great and Little Bourton were dependent on the parent church of Cropredy, up to two miles away, and Nonconformity flourished.

The rebuilders in the sixties incorporated whatever they could of the old church in the new, but inevitably there is little of the original to be seen outside the chancel with its Decorated east window and piscina. Some carved stones are the only identifiable parts of the old nave.

Near the church, Manor House and Friar's Cottage have stonework carrying the date 1685.

HANWELL

A WINDING LANE off the winding road through the village of attractive ironstone cottages leads to the church and a sudden recollection of Hampton Court. Hanwell Castle, as built in the reign of Henry VII, had four towers, but the one that remains, castellated and in red brick, is sufficient reminder of the more famous Tudor residence;

Bell Tower, All Saints, Great Bourton

and Hanwell also entertained royalty. The church as it is today was built almost two centuries before the castle, and an earlier church two centuries before that, but just as castle and church are combined in a glance, so for the past five hundred years they have been associated, and were for some time physically linked.

The church today, the product of 14th century re-building, retains some earlier work, notably the north and south Early English doorways, and the massive Norman font carved with intersecting arcading. The most notable feature, however, is the array of sculpture on the capitals of the nave arcades and on the external cornices of the north and south walls of the chancel. Some capitals are encircled by male and female figures with arms intertwined, surmounted by amusing figures of musicians, while the cornices are alive with grotesques, forming a gallery of natural and unnatural creation.

A first impression of the interior is of ample space, which may have encouraged Cromwell's men to stable their horses here. Nave and aisles were much the same then as now, with the clerestory added to give extra height and light. Neither men nor animals would respect

Hanwell Castle

St. Peter, Hanwell

monuments, decorations or windows. The worn re-cumbent effigy of a woman, part of a 14th century tomb in the floor of the south aisle, would be particularly vulnerable, and the five weeping figures in the reredos

under the east window of the north aisle only rather less so, while the comparative splendour of the Cope mon-ument would be a great temptation.

A second impression is of the unusual height of the

Parliament a revised version of the Book of Common Prayer. He entertained James I twice here at Hanwell and now occupies the impressive tomb in the chancel.

The good condition of Hanwell Church today and the careful preservation of its historic features owe much to the generosity of The Friends of the Oxfordshire Churches. Hanwell was the first church they restored, in 1970.

HEMPTON

ABOUT A MILE and a half to the west of Deddington, the hamlet of Hempton shares with Clifton a special relationship with the mother parish (page 17). But un-like Clifton it stands on a ridge, hence the 'Hempton high way' of the rhyme, which is also the highway from Deddington to Chipping Norton.

The church stands on the north side of the road and resembles Clifton church in standing as a monument to a parson's generosity. This was Rev. William Wilson, a rector of Over Worton, the small village about two miles to the south. It was built at his expense, and in it he installed Over Worton's Norman font. Simple in shape this is decorated all over with chevrons, and is Hempton's one link with the distant past.

The architect of the church was the rector's son, another Rev. William Wilson, and a Deddington builder was employed. The church is in Gothic style, comprising nave, chancel, north aisle and porch, with a cote for a single bell on the west gable. The building was dedicated in 1851 and, until other accommodation could be provided, the aisle was used as a school room.

HORLEY

HORLEY CHURCH IS an education. It stands four-square on top of a hill on which clings the golden-stoned village,

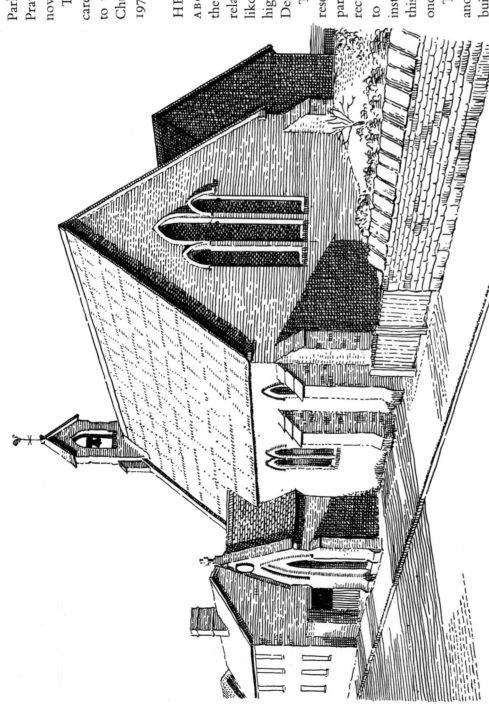

St. John the Evangelist, Hempton

chancel floor: this was raised when the Cope family vault was constructed beneath it in 1776. The Copes continue to dominate the chancel with the large, hand-some alabaster monument supporting the recumbent figures of Sir Anthony and his wife, and with memorials on the opposite wall and brasses in the floor.

William Cope, cofferer to Henry VII, built Hanwell Castle, linking it to the chancel of the church by a gallery. His son, the first Sir Anthony Cope, was vice-chamber-lain to Queen Catherine Parr and grandfather to the second Sir Anthony, a famous Puritan, who when MP for Banbury was sent to the Tower for presenting to

St. Etheldreda, Horley

27

St. John the Baptist, Hornton

and one is led to it by its embattled central tower and attracted towards its three very fine Early English door-ways. Two of the doors are unlocked, and to push open either is to encounter a flash of the mediaeval church. Leisurely scrutiny does not lead to disappointment: it provides the rich experience of a mediaeval church perhaps as complete as one can reasonably expect after the inevitable deterioration, renovation and restoration of centuries.

Enter by the south door and you are faced like the parishioners of old with a large wall painting of St. Christopher, though unlike them you will hardly be affected by the superstition that having seen it you will be safe for the day from sudden or accidental death. But the fresco is unusually striking and complete, though reinforced by retouching, and you can read the words of the saint and the Child as readily as you can pick out two successful anglers at the foot, fishing by the light of the stars.

Enter by the door in the handsome west front and you take in the bright chancel, the two arches supporting the central tower, and the spacious nave and aisles, while the imaginatively reconstructed rood loft and screen complete with figures are undeniably impressive. Four architectural periods are harmonised: the Norman walls of the chancel, and the tub font: the Early English pillars and arches of the nave and tower: the decorated windows in the chancel and south aisle: and the perpendicular windows of the north aisle.

The colours of the rood loft are seen again in the pulpit, painted during the major restoration of the church (about 1950), and, more authentically, in the St. Christopher and the remains of two other wall paintings: one on the pillar by the font, thought to represent St. Etheldreda, patron saint of the church; and the other on the north wall by the chancel arch, comprising a pattern of rings each enclosing the letter 't' possibly the initial of Thomas

à Becket, Archbishop of Canterbury, martyred 1170. Colour also gleams in the old glass of two windows in the north aisle depicting two 15th century rectors and the east window of the south aisle showing the shield of the Beauchamp arms.

Among the church's other treasures are two brasses beneath the tower representing six girls – the brasses of their parents and their brothers have been removed. And contrasting with the strength of the church's exterior, a touching memorial set in its south wall to Ursula, wife of James, and their infant who died in 1696, witnesses to life's fragility.

HORNTON

OF ALL THE picture-book villages of North Oxfordshire many people would give Hornton first place. Lying in the bottom of a valley, it begins to captivate any visitor as soon as he descends, and captivation is complete as he stands under the trees on the green with the village round him. In full view is the 17th century thatched manor house, but the church, just visible at the end of a narrow lane, is seen at its best from the hill to the south. With church and village built of the same gold-rich Hornton stone, once quarried here but now some miles away, the panorama is a patchwork of gold and green, thatch and slate.

Now well cared for, the church gives no hint that less than a century ago it was in such bad repair that weeds flourished in it. Had it been respected in earlier days – and its walls not covered with limewash at the time of Cromwell – its 14th century wall paintings would have provided a brilliant gallery. They richly decorated the whole of the south aisle, where hardly a trace now remains, and covered the wall above the chancel arch with a 'Doom', of which sufficent remains of the pale animated

figures on their sombre ground to make this wall paint-ing one of the best known in the county. Traces of later paintings in the north aisle and on the wall of the chancel can also be seen.

The nucleus of the present church was built late in the 12th century as can be seen in the nave, north aisle and triple-arched nave arcade with its piers and capitals typical of the period. The font, carved with interlacing arches and with rows of cable moulding at the base, is of the same period. During the next two centuries the church was enlarged and reconstructed, notably by the addition of a clerestory and south aisle and by alteration of doorways and windows, generally bringing it to the shape we now see, although inevitably some of the work of these centuries has been altered or lost. Of the chapel that opened off the north side of the chancel, only a walled-up arch remains. The tower dates from the 14th or possibly the 15th, century which also gave the east end of the chancel its present character.

Brasses of the 16th century in the floor of the chancel and south aisle are usual reminders of mortality, but it is the eerie, excited figures of the Last Judgment that one remembers. Yet there is a message of hope in the lines of a memorial to five children of one family who died in infancy, almost hidden on the outside west wall of the church.

Figures from the Doom, Hornton

St. Laurence, Milcombe

MOLLINGTON

ON ITS HILL and screened by trees, Mollington Church is glimpsed from the main road and then lost on the steep descent into the village which hangs on the hillside and enjoys broad views over into Warwickshire. Recent building has much changed the character of the village whose old houses, mostly of local stone and thatch, kept happier company with the church.

There has been a church here at least since the early 13th century, as the font with its dog-tooth ornament shows. The earliest parts of the present structure, from the 14th century, are the chancel and nave with its four arches leading into the north aisle, the moulding of each arch ending in a carved head. Traces of the same period are found in the porch, which was rebuilt in 1715 using the old materials.

The original north aisle was demolished in 1786 but rebuilt in 1855 when the church was extensively restored. In the intervening years the arches were blocked up like the one to be seen on the north side of the chancel today. The aisle probably continued behind this, terminating in a chapel which was demolished about the same time, for a piscina and a blocked-up doorway can be seen in the chancel's outside wall.

During restoration, the somewhat roughly carved chancel screen, painted with the Crosses of Lancaster and York, was moved to its present position beneath the tower arch.

The tower itself is of the early 16th century, the mouldings on its west window incorporating figures, now time-worn, which have been identified as a lion, a dragon and an angel.

To see Mollington Church, which has been quite lately lovingly restored, glowing with daffodils for the Easter festival, with home-painted eggs among moss and

MILCOMBE

IT MUST BE annoying for any resident of Milcombe scanning the guide books for information on the church to find, time and again, that greater prominence is given to a dovecote, however handsome the dovecote may be, and unquestionably the one built for Milcombe Hall in the 18th century is noteworthy.

The church is usually written off because of its extensive remodelling by the Victorians, but much work of earlier centuries remains and to the worshipper the building imparts its own atmosphere. It is essentially in the Decorated style, but the north aisle is separated from the nave by a plain Early English arcade, with cylindrical pillars and plain moulded capitals.

The chancel screen is Perpendicular, of the 15th century, and beautifully carved, though much restored. The ends of the benches installed during this period were also finely carved, with a variegated tracery, and pieces have been kept. They can be seen mounted on the east wall of the north aisle. From the 15th century also comes the font, comprising a very shallow bowl on a simple stem.

The tower, at the west end of the nave, is of the 14th century with a plain Decorated doorway and belfry windows that have only very recently been blocked-up windows that have only very recently been blocked up (since the drawing was done) to replace badly broken louvres.

Three windows of the 14th and 15th centuries that were removed from the church during the major restoration of 1860 were used in the village school then being built. This has now been converted into a village hall, so part of the old church survives here too.

MILTON

MANY VILLAGES IN Oxfordshire, as elsewhere, have an inn next door or very near to the church. But there can be few where the inn was there first – by two centuries. It is true of Milton. This hamlet – the 'middletown' between Adderbury and Bloxham – boasts the 'Black Boy' which retains part of the structure and some details of the original 16th and 17th century building. The church was not built until 1856–7 and there is no sign of the earlier chapel (unless it is the 14th century doorway built into one of the cottages) or of the Presbyterian church which signalled the importance that Milton briefly achieved as a centre of Nonconformity two hundred years ago.

The present church with its distinctive red-tiled central tower was designed in Early Decorated style by William Butterfield, architect of Keble College, Oxford and All Saints, Margaret Street, London, noted for his highly ornate effects achieved with different coloured bricks, marble and mosaics. Such effects are hardly to be seen at Milton which is among his early work. By no means flamboyant it is a small, pleasant church, comprising nave and chancel and is entered through a lych gate and porch entirely in character. It is difficult to understand why one guide book to Oxfordshire could describe the church as ugly.

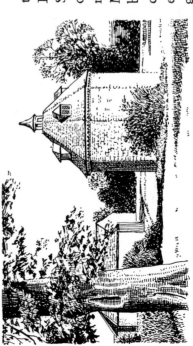

Dovecote, Milcombe

Holy Trinity, Shenington

34

wild flowers on the window ledges, and with an Easter garden in a corner of the north aisle, is to see the small English country church at its most appealing.

SHENINGTON

SHENINGTON CHURCH, WHICH has shared its rector with Alkerton since 1900, looks across to its sister church from one hilltop to another. Between them is Sor Brook and a steep winding road that leads up to the village green across which the church is seen, its Hornton stone matching the houses round it.

There has been a church here since early in the 12th century and one of its fine features remains. It is the Norman arch framing the organ pipes in the north wall of the chancel. Ornamented with rows of chevrons and cable moulding, and its capitals carved with stars and scrolls, it must have looked even more splendid in its original position as the chancel arch before the church was restored a century ago. The capitals of the Early English arcade between the nave and south aisle are also carved, more intricately, with faces, flowers and foliage and are supported by octagonal piers on high plain bases. Above are clerestory windows of the 14th century. Faces also gaze from the corbels of the nave roof and the base of the 15th century tower.

A more intriguing sculpture is seen on the outside wall of the aisle. Here, in a Decorated niche, is a figure with hands raised, possibly in blessing, and by his side is an ox. Whatever its significance, it does not look incongruous in this rural environment, or as a decoration on one of the few churches which maintains its custom – at least two hundred years old – of grass strewing. Here the floor is strewn with grass each year for three weeks beginning Whit Sunday.

Shenington Church seen across the village green

The man and the ox have been mute witnesses of many developments over the past six hundred years, but none more spectacular or epoch-making then the one in 1942, when the first aircraft powered by Frank Whittle's jet engine took off from the nearby airfield. Here began the jet age; but the airfield, laid down at the beginning of the war, is now a go-kart racing track.

SHUTFORD

TO MANY PEOPLE in the Banbury area, Shutford is still associated with plush, although the mill closed twenty-five years ago. In this tiny village deep in rolling country, plush weaving was quite literally a rural industry which came and went within about two centuries, its decline being hastened by the decline of the royal courts of Europe who used Shutford plush for flunkeys' liveries. For all the wide acres around, church, manor house and inn are crowded upon each other. The visitor is led by the pinnacled 15th century tower which appears poised above the inn but is almost dwarfed by the tower of the manor house on the edge of the churchyard.

The church, of appealing simplicity, is largely of the 13th and 14th centuries, but the nave arcade with its pointed arches goes back to the 12th century, and the octagonal font with its tall arcading is of the same period. An unusual feature is the small north chapel built as a transept at an angle of more than ninety degrees to the aisle opening into it. With its deep-set lancet windows, the chapel is of the 13th century, and probably the chancel was built about the same time, its dark oak screen being installed two centuries later.

The church was restored, with some rebuilding, at various times in the last century, during which extensive remains of early wall paintings (mentioned by Beesley) were lost. One imagines these being lively and colourful, contrasting with the rather sombre exterior presented to the village chiefly by the prominent west wall with its two small windows, one of which is a tiny Romanesque window beneath the tower. Similarly, the manor house exterior would give no hint of the activity in one of its big rooms just before the Civil War, when Lord Saye and Sele drilled his troops here in secret.

SIBFORD

THIS PARISH, COMPRISING Sibford Gower with Burdrop and Sibford Ferris facing each other across a gully of one of the Stour's tributaries, is popularly associated with the Quakers, through their celebrated school, their burial ground and their history. The history of the Church in this place is, by comparison, unknown, perhaps because the parish church at Sibford Gower, erected in 1840, gives no hint of it, not even in the ground it stands on. Yet there was a chapel at Sibford Gower before 1153 and by the end of the century it had its own burial ground. Originally granted to the Templars, the chapel eventually passed to the hospitallers and for some time was independent of the mother church of Swalcliffe and had its own curate.

However, about the mid-16th century the rough stone building was in ruins, and it was another three hundred years before the people of Sibford again had a church of their own. The ground was given by the Rev. William Gilkes and the cost of building met by public subscription. Designed by an Oxford architect H. J. Underwood, the church is in Early English style comprising nave, transepts and small chancel, with a porch added in 1879. The unstained choir stalls, which are a feature of the interior, and a new organ, were presented by parishioners in 1906, while another kind of devotion is commemorated in a memorial window to Flying Officer Hugh Oddie who died in 1943.

St. Martin, Shutford

Holy Trinity, Sibford

SOUTH NEWINGTON

THE PAST HUNDRED YEARS are so often charged with having obscured, or lost, so many glories from a church's past through insensitive restoration that it is particularly satisfying to record the example of South Newington as a church whose treasures have been brought to light within the past half century.

Writing in 1823, Skelton selects the porch as most worthy of note, but locally – and farther afield too – the church is now best known for its 14th century wall paintings, the most remarkable of which were uncovered by Professor E. W. Tristram in 1931.

One of this impressive gallery is believed to be unique as the only representation of its subject in English art – the martyrdom of Thomas, Earl of Lancaster. Alongside it, on the north wall, is the better known subject of the martyrdom of St. Thomas of Canterbury, and while much of both murals has inevitably been lost, the beautifully drawn figure of each martyr is virtually complete. This is particularly surprising in the case of Thomas à Becket, since Henry VIII ordered that all memorials to him should be obliterated. The mural of this subject in the church of North Stoke in the south of the county was not so fortunate.

St. Peter ad Vincula, South Newington

38

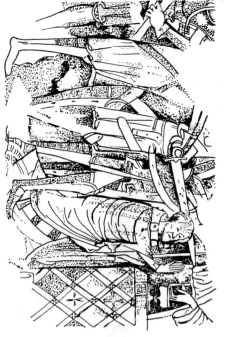

Martyrdom of Thomas à Becket, South Newington

On the same wall, beyond a deeply set window which has other – less easily decipherable – paintings on the side of it, is one of the most appealing of all the pictures, showing a graceful Madonna and Child, with kneeling saints. High on the north arcade are the remains of eighteen scenes from the Passion painted a century later; some of these have disappeared altogether, but, of the remainder, one showing the Entry into Jerusalem is particularly bold and attractive. A big disappointment is the Doom over the chancel arch; painted about the year 1375, it is, alas, almost unrecognisable.

In frames round the walls are numerous Royal Proclamations, including one deploring the 'execrable murder of Our Royal Father Charles the First' and ordering a day of fast and humiliation in his memory. There are also affidavits required by the Act for Burial in Woollen 1677 testifying that bodies were shrouded and coffins lined in sheep's wool, as a means of boosting the woollen trade. One of several wall tablets is to the memory of the district nurse.

The church fabric successfully combines the work of several periods. The south porch is Perpendicular in style, finely proportioned and pinnacled, matching the pinnacled tower which is mainly of the 14th century. The nave arcades are of the 13th century with variously shaped pillars, capitals and bases, except that the two centre bays of the north arcade are Norman. The deeply set windows of the north aisle are Decorated with flowing tracery and those of the south aisle include Early English, Decorated and early Perpendicular. The nave clerestory is Perpendicular, of the 15th century. The chancel beyond the plain Early English chancel arch is mainly 14th century with a Decorated piscina, and among the old glass in its windows are four roundels with emblems of the Evangelists. Fragments of old glass are also to be found in the windows of the north aisle, showing human heads, animals and birds.

The font is Norman, having a plain cylindrical bowl with a zigzag pattern incised round the lip. Of the many people baptised in it over the centuries, one can envy most (if only momentarily) those who saw the church in its painted glory.

SWALCLIFFE

OF ALL THE interesting features of this church, the chief must be the pair of partly blocked-up round-headed windows facing each other high across the nave. Uncomfortably placed and unexciting in appearance, they are noteworthy nevertheless as evidence of the small Saxon church built on this spot over nine centuries ago. Parts of its walls were later incorporated in a Norman church, of which there remain the three rounded arches, supported by cylindrical columns with square capitals, at the west end of the north arcade. The three semi-pointed arches on octagonal columns in the arcade opposite were built almost a century later.

Throughout that century – 13th – the church was much enlarged, chiefly by the addition of the aisles and chancel. At the same time, the porch was built and also the lower part of the tower with its three stout arches and very deep-set window in the west wall. Considerable alterations were made in the following century, comprising chiefly the addition of the clerestory and the rebuilding of the north aisle, and it is from this period that the font comes, the rough carving round its rim being painted red, white and blue by some 17th century enthusiast for colour.

Repair and renovation continued throughout the 15th century. The tower was altered and raised to its present height, the chancel was remodelled and the screen installed beneath its wide arch. It was then just as it is today with its painted and gilded decoration and its double gates on the same hinges. In Elizabethan times it was probably surmounted by the painted timber scroll work that is now used as a screen at the west end of the south aisle.

The 17th century was a time of refurbishing and essential repair both to the fabric and furnishings. New woodwork was added to chancel and nave – the two front pews of which carry the dates 1637 and 1638 – while the pulpit and lectern were presented in 1639 by Anne Wykeham, who is depicted in painted stone with her husband on a canopied monument against the wall of the north aisle. Over centuries the Wykehams had a residence in Swalcliffe, and it is to William of Wykeham that the village owes its famous tithe barn near the church.

In a profusion of stained glass there is a window in the chancel, above the priest's stall, which was presented by the clergy of the deanery. It commemorates the kindness shown to many of them by Canon E. J. Payne, rural dean in the late 1870s.

The delicate light from stained-glass adds mystery to the Wykeham tomb and two other canopied tombs of the

SS Peter and Paul, Swalcliffe

40

16th and 17th centuries, also to a coffin in the floor by the south wall, and the remains of three wall paintings. Other items of interest are an oak chest, tilting helmets (now kept in the priest's vestry since part of one was stolen) and a fire hook once used to pull burning thatch from roofs.

The spaciousness of the church as it is today – and no doubt its preservation – is due to the restoration work of the last century, when the whole of the west end was opened up. Here is an impressive church for a small village which it oversees from its height on the Banbury to Shipston road.

TADMARTON

ABOUT A MILE of undulating road from Swalcliffe is the church of Tadmarton, also on the roadside but partly hidden by trees. There was a Norman church here on much the same plan as the present one, and remains of it can be seen in the three simple arches of the north nave arcade, in the two blocked arches in the north wall of the chancel and in the stonework of the window opposite.

But the legacy of the 13th century remains the more vivid, represented most strikingly by the font. Grotesque heads, with ballflowers between them, support the bowl, its four sides crowded with a variety of sculptured ornament – overlapping circles, tracery, foliage and scrolls – supported by a decorated octagonal shaft. At this period the church was enlarged: the chancel was rebuilt and given a new arch, the nave was also rebuilt and extended, and the fine north doorway with its clustered shafts and foliated capitals was installed. The lower part of the tower was also erected, to be extended to its present height two hundred years later, when the original belfry windows were filled in. Also in the 15th

St. Nicholas, Tadmarton

St. Mary Magdalene, Wardington

42

century, the clerestory was added to the nave, Perpendicular tracery inserted in the Early English windows, and the sanctus bell turret added to the east gable of the nave.

Thus the church evolved much as we now see it, although every century made its mark on fabric and furnishings, such as the finely carved mediaeval benches to be found in the nave. And at the close of the much maligned last century the church 'sadly fallen into decay' was generally restored and hidden beauties were revealed.

WARDINGTON

WARDINGTON IS ONE of the villages that the motorist races through on his way to Daventry and the Mr. But it is a pleasant village that would repay a visit, with its old thatched cottages, its manor house and, only a few yards off the main road, its church.

The church that can incorporate in its furnishings the handiwork of its parishioners is fortunate. Such work represents and offers the skill and labour of all its people, just as the congregation meeting week by week represents them in person. In Wardington the reredos in the chancel and the oak front of the altar have been elaborately carved by one pair of village hands (those of a crippled lady), and the lectern has been carved in fine detail by the village carpenter (who was also responsible for the lectern at Mollington). Curiously, if Beesley's comment is accepted, the church building in 1841 (that is, before restoration in 1887 and 1889) was something of a local effort too, being 'from the plainness and even rudeness of the work ... palpably the work of country builders in imitation of some neighbouring church'. But that comment would hardly be made today.

The church is entered through a fine Early English doorway, with a stoup on the right, into nave and aisles of the same period. The low arches of the nave arcades are supported by plain round pillars except for three clustered columns in the south arcade. The capital of one of these facing the door is surmounted by the heads of a bishop and a hare. It is thought that the south aisle, with a chapel at the east end, was built rather earlier than the north aisle, which is wider – possibly owing to the presence of a 12th century transept. A trace of this can be seen at the east end of the nave arcade, while evidence of this earlier church is also to be found in a partially blocked up window in the chancel.

The clerestory was added in the 14th century, although its two large windows on the south side are of a century later. Early in the 14th century the windows in the chancel and the east end of the north aisle were replaced by the present windows in Decorated style. Some years later the tower was built, and later still, in the 15th century, the vestry was added–with a loft which was removed in 1915.

In this setting can be found numerous items of interest from various centuries. The chancel screen, and its counterparts between the chapel and the chancel and between the chapel and the south aisle, have mediaeval tracery. The octagonal font bears in its panels the legend 'RMRS 1666'. In the floor of the south aisle, beneath an arch in the wall, there is a mediaeval coffin stone curiously carved with a head and hands in prayer, and a floor brass commemorates a gentleman who died in 1444. The chapel has a variety of memorials – in the floor, on the walls and most notably in the east window which was formerly blocked up and has been restored as a memorial to John, Lord Wardington who died in 1950. The chapel was restored by George Loveday, then of the Manor House. It has another very attractive window depicting episodes in the parable of the Good Samaritan.

The good pulpit and the stained glass in the little round window above the chancel arch were the gift of Rev. D. J. Welburn (Vicar 1887–1913) in whose time the church was restored.

There is yet another memorial worthy of mention, in the chancel: this is the reredos, which was not only made by local hands but also commemorates one man's fifty years as vicar's warden. It is a further reminder of parishioners' service to their church, like the altar front and the lectern.

WIGGINTON

WIGGINTON STANDING AT THE edge of the village, the church is still very much part of it, with its dark ironstone walls weathered outside but clean and fresh within. For a small place, it has much of interest. Curiosity is roused at the entrance which is through a porch uniquely placed at an angle facing the village, at the west end of the north aisle. Inside the door are two old chests, the one on the left being the original parish chest of the 16th century. But one's eyes are first attracted to the unspoilt body of the church, the nave and aisles with their Early English arcading lit by fine triple-lancet windows of the same period and by Perpendicular square-headed windows of the 15th century clerestory. The high roof of the nave is very fine, some of its bosses carved with 15th century sun and rose devices, and below them, on each side, a gallery of carved stone heads.

Facing the chancel, one notices in the east wall of the north aisle a doorway giving access to stairs that formerly led to the rood loft. The chancel itself is in the Decorated style, the product of rebuilding in the first half of the 14th century. It is lit by six windows containing fragments of old glass, including two low-sided windows (originally used for ventilation), one at each side. Beside the one in the south wall, and let into the back of the chancel arch, is a seat with an arched canopy elegantly crocketed and

St. Giles, Wigginton

44

decorated. One of the church's curiosities, this canopy could once have been part of a row of sedilia adjacent to the piscina in the south wall. The decoration includes carvings of a swan and dolphin, heraldic devices recalling Henry V and his queen, Katharine of France (married in 1420) and, curiously enough, paralleled in names of the village's two inns.

Opposite each other, very low in the chancel walls, are arched recesses with recumbent effigies. The mutilated figure on the north side, of an early 14th century knight, formerly occupied the recess in the south wall from which it was removed in 1870 to make way for the three figures now occupying it. This group, comprising a large central figure with purse and sword and two female figures to a smaller scale, formerly stood upright against the outside wall of the south aisle: why, is one the church's mysteries.

As can be seen from a drawing hanging in the church, the chancel had a clerestory similar in style to that over the nave and probably erected at the same time, but it was dismantled during extensive restoration in 1871. The tower was probably built about the same time as the clerestories, or possibly earlier.

There were periods in the past three centuries when the church fabric was in very poor condition – indeed in 1668 the churchwardens were threatened with excommunication for not repairing it – and the care and taste with which the work of three architectural periods has been retained in the present building is cause for gratitude.

The church, however, is essentially people, not buildings, and no record of St. Giles, Wigginton could be complete without reference to the 50 years' service of its latest – and possibly last – rector, the late Canon A. J. S.

Hart (incumbent 1922–1973 and sometime Rural Dean) whose devotion to the parish and its church has left its imprint on the history of both.

Canon Hart was surely one of the most dedicated in a long succession of rectors of Wigginton stretching back to the 13th century. A list of them hangs in the church – a commonplace feature which the regular worshipper takes for granted, but which invariably fascinates the visitor to an old church. The mutilated names of the early centuries evoke past ages more vividly than the church's fabric and one sometimes finds American visitors writing them down.

As records show, Canon Hart's predecessors over the centuries were inevitably a mixture of the conscientious and the indolent. The latter were largely a consequence of poor benefice endowment, which was not uncommon, and meant that many of the rectors did not reside in the parish but hired poorly-paid curates to do the work, some of whom did not live in the parish either.

One of the more active of Wigginton's curates was Charles Winstanley who in 1824 uncovered the remains of a Roman villa while carrying out excavations about 200 yards from the east end of the church. These were ploughed over, until excavations undertaken by the Ministry of Works in 1965 again uncovered them, bringing to light the remains of fifteen rooms and ten mosaic floors. The villa was judged to have been built in the 3rd century, so Wigginton has been a settlement for at least seventeen hundred years, being served for about half that time by a Christian church.

THE WORTONS

WHEN YOU ARE in the Wortons you are really in the country. Here in the rolling farmlands of Oxfordshire, where one is much aware of the pictures made by sky and trees, one hamlet nestles in the valley while the other occupies the hill, as their names imply. The two churches, separated by less than a mile as the crow flies, and by two centuries or more, are set among trees.

Trees dwarf the church at *Nether Worton*, one of the smallest and most intimate in North Oxfordshire, with surely the smallest-ever chancel. It stands on the opposite side of the lane to a stately Jacobean manor house which once had a moat, of which only a pond-like stretch of water is a reminder. The church is in Decorated style with an Early English doorway at the foot of a simple square tower erected during extensive rebuilding of the church in the 17th century. For all its size, there are two aisles, extremely narrow, separated from the nave by arcades having wide capitals.

The church is unusual in having a school and schoolhouse attached to it, making three buildings in a row. A door in the west wall leads into the schoolroom which is not now used as such.

A wall monument by Henry Westmacott commemorates a dedicated pastor, Rev. William Wilson (died 1821 one of whose descendants, Grace Wilson, produced the large drawing of Christ bearing the Cross which decorates the north wall.

The church has a minor place in history as the first of many old churches in Britain to be re-roofed in aluminium in 1952. This modern material, rolled in Banbury, replaced the old perished lead which had a scrap value high enough to cover the cost of the new roof.

The church of *Over Worton*, almost enclosed by trees but with lovely vistas from its position above the valley is, in contrast, Victorian – or 'rich Victorian' to use John Betjeman's words. It incorporates a chancel arch of the 13th century and 14th century windows, and once had a Norman font which was moved to Hempton. At the east end of the small south aisle there is a fine effigy of an

Since the above was written, Wigginton has been placed in the care of the vicar of Hook Norton, in the neighbouring deanery.

St. James, Nether Worton

46

Elizabethan gentleman which was discovered under the the floor boards a few years ago. He is dressed in legal robes and may well be Edmund Meese to whom there is a memorial tablet in Latin. He was connected with the Law and lived at Over Worton where he was lord of the manor.

Over Worton also has a claim to fame. About twenty years before the church was rebuilt, the future Cardinal Newman preached his first sermon here ten days after being made deacon at Oxford. The incumbent of Over Worton at the time had been the schoolmaster responsible for Newman's spiritual conversion at the age of fifteen. He preached from the text 'Man goeth forth to his work and to his labour until the evening', which was to be the text of his final sermon as an Anglican priest nineteen years later.

WROXTON

THE VIEW OF Wroxton's thatched cottages grouped round the village pond is one of the most familiar in books on villages of England. Almost as familiar is the imposing gabled front of Wroxton Abbey, seen across wide lawns and framed by the tall trees of an extensive park. Grandeur and simplicity living together, and the church serving both. But with the 'abbey' now a college, the nobility are no longer present in the pews, only in the tombs.

It is a good 14th century Decorated church with nothing in the fabric from an earlier building and with later additions all of a piece with the original. For the nave clerestory and the roof over the aisles are from a century later and the tower was redesigned and entirely rebuilt in the 18th century. The windows have a simple tracery, yet the east window with its five lights is undeniably impressive.

The chancel screen is lavishly ornamented with

Holy Trinity, Over Worton

All Saints, Wroxton

carvings, including a representation of Abraham pre-
paring to sacrifice Isaac, and the fine 14th century font is
encircled by carved figures of six apostles, the Virgin, and
possibly the woman of Samaria. Indeed, carving in wood
and stone is the church's glory. The carved woodwork
(in high relief) of the pulpit, the reredos and the choir
stalls is by continental craftsmen of the 16th and 17th
centuries, presented by Col. North of Wroxton Abbey,
who gave similar carvings to the daughter church at
Balscote. He was so enchanted by such woodwork,
which he probably obtained from Flanders and Italy,
that he used it exuberantly in all manner of ways throughout the abbey during its restoration and extension in
1858, and he was similarly enthusiastic about having it
installed in the church.

Here it is outshone, however, by the carved monuments, especially the Pope tomb which almost indecently
dominates the sanctuary. Sir William Pope, 1st Earl of

Downe, built the house known as the abbey, on the site of a mediaeval priory. There he entertained King James I and there he died in 1631, and he and his wife now lie in canopied magnificence in the church, attended by their three kneeling children, superbly carved in alabaster.

A later occupant of the abbey, Lord North, the Prime Minister, is also buried here with numerous members of his family, including other Earls of Guildford. He is commemorated in the chancel, in a wall slab by Flaxman showing Britannia with a lion at her feet. The church has many other memorials and gravestones, one of the latter marking the grave of Thomas Coutts, founder of the banking house, and there are some brasses, including one of 1557.

In his book of antiquities, Skelton records two verses paying tribute to the peace and contentment of the village, which he found inscribed on one of the cottages. The last lines apply with special poignancy to the church, with its many memorials to the great:

Peace spreads around her balmy wings,
And, banished from the courts of Kings
Has fixed her mansion here.

Wroxton village pond

49

St. Michael, Aynho

Some Northamptonshire Churches

AYNHO

THE SOUTHERNMOST of Northamptonshire villages, Aynho is also one of the prettiest, a hill village of thatched stone cottages with roses framing the doors and apricot trees climbing the walls. The cottages, with unfenced gardens, line one side of the sharply twisting Banbury-London road, facing the village stocks on a triangle of green, the gateway to the manor house Aynho Park, and the half-concealed opening to the lane leading past the 17th century rectory to the church.

While almost every old church is a combination of styles accumulated through centuries of addition, restoration and rebuilding, but only recognisable as such by the architecturally curious, it is true to say that St. Michael's, Aynho would strike anybody as a mixture, and a very unusual one. The tower is clearly in one style above the door, must have been outstandingly impressive domestic than ecclesiastical, matching the architecture of the manor house nearby.

The Cartwrights, lords of the manor of Aynho for about three centuries, were Parliamentarians during the Civil War and the house was burned down by Royalists after their defeat at Naseby in 1645. The house was almost entirely rebuilt some fifty years later (to be remodelled by Sir John Soane in 1800) and in 1725 the body of the church was rebuilt to match it, retaining the 15th century tower. The architect was a native of Aynho, Edward

and the remainder of the church in another, a style more and a very unusual one. The tower is clearly in one style though it is now, with a good richly traceried window when the niches in the diagonal buttresses held the figures of two saints on one side and St. Michael slaying the Devil on the other.

As might be expected, the church contains many memorials to the Cartwrights, but there is none, alas, to the last Cartwright to be lord of the manor, who delighted to show visitors round his house with its fine collection of pictures and ceramics. Both he and his heir, a boy in his teens, were killed in a car accident in 1954 and their burial service was held at St. John's RC Church,

Wing, formerly employed as a carpenter at Aynho Park and with a number of London churches to his credit, Pevsner suggests that since the influence of Thomas Archer, who worked on the architecture of the church, he may well have had a hand in designing it. Beesley describes the result as 'one of the tasteless compositions of the period; it has been often likened to a gentleman's stables' -- an extreme view, perhaps because the church is something of a curiosity, unique in the area.

The interior, though somewhat unexciting in its rectangular shape, is undeniably light and spacious, with a fine west gallery on Tuscan columns (a reminder of Aynho Park), a Georgian pulpit and box pews, and it gains much by being well kept. The tower, very fine remain, but the house with its impressive 17th century porch and its collection of pictures, furniture and silver is of much interest and is open to the public.

The church, standing some distance away in a beautiful setting among trees at the end of a winding lane, was once served by the priory, and following the suppression by Henry VIII became a vicariate. The priory and demesne lands were granted to one Michael Fox of London in 1543 in repayment of a loan. An unusual brass, now much worn, commemorating this same 'Myghell Fox Cytyzen & Groc of London' is to be found in the chancel.

The church is largely of the 14th century, good Decorated but much restored. It is entered through a fine

Banbury. For the Cartwright of the previous generation had adopted the Roman Catholic faith on marrying an Italian wife and the family's link with Aynho church was broken. The house is now used as flats, with many of its treasures still in place.

CHACOMBE

IN TERMS OF historical interest, Chacombe is invariably associated with the Priory, the beautiful house built in the 17th and 18th centuries on the site of a priory established early in the 13th century for Canons Regular of St. Augustine. Apart from the chapel, which has recently been restored, only fragments of the original priory

south porch stone-vaulted and without timber like the bigger south porch of the sister church of Middleton Cheney. The studded double door retains its mediaeval ironwork, opening to show the church's oldest possession, a Norman font ringed by a cable coil and an arcade of intersecting arches. It stands on the right before a pillar on which is incised a small mitred head above a cross. The pillars supporting the low arches of each nave arcade are octagonal, curiously capped by disproportionately wide quatrefoiled capitals. Above them are carved heads terminating the labels over the arches. The clerestory windows are different on each side, being squareheaded on the south and small quatrefoils on the north. There is a piscina not only in the chancel but also in the east wall of both north and south aisles, reminders of former chapels and of the days when the church was more fully used serving an active priory.

All the bells in the tower were cast in Chacombe at the Bagley foundry, now defunct, which was responsible for many church bells in the district and indeed throughout the country. Henry Bagley, the master founder, died in 1684 and is buried in the churchyard. His memory is kept alive by the inscription on some of the bells he cast: 'Henry Bagley made me'.

CROUGHTON

BANBURY AREA IS favoured, and perhaps does not know it, in having close at hand two such wonderful displays of mediaeval wall paintings as are to be found in the churches of South Newington and Croughton. Enthusiasts for this type of art, while recognising different styles and periods, may argue the claims of one over the other, but would agree that in both there are the remnants

SS Peter and Paul, Chacombe

of most distinguished work, important to the study of wall paintings of the 13th and 14th centuries.

Croughton's finest are thought to have been painted about 1300 when they must have been a magnificent sight covering almost completely the walls of the nave and two aisles. To these were added a century or so later a Last Judgment over the chancel arch and other paintings round the clerestory. Marvelling that any part of such paintings could survive repeated plastering-over from the Reformation onwards, and acknowledging again one's gratitude to Professor Tristram who un-covered them in 1923-24, when they caused great excite-ment in the parish, one yet feels disappointment at not having seen them at the time of their restoration. This was before they were waxed over for protection, only to become dirty and damp and then lose much of their colour when the wax was removed.

Presenting in thirty-six episodes the Birth and Passion of Christ and the Life of the Virgin, the complete paint-ings would offer a picture narrative of valuable instruction (despite the number of apocryphal episodes) and almost endless fascination, for the scenes are depicted in rich and curious detail. Such details would evoke immediate response: thus, the Birth takes place in a bed with a red cover and white sheets, and the Wise Men are on horses not camels. The favourite scene may well have been, as it probably still is on account of its appealing subject and good condition, the Flight into Egypt, while the Last Supper, which is also well preserved, draws its eternal response as the origin of the Church's supreme celebra-tion, which it has always felt the need to illustrate, from the simplest pictorial statement on a tomb in the Cata-combs to the profound representation of Leonardo. We can believe that The Massacre of the Innocents and scenes from the Passion and Crucifixion would have an awe-some effect on 14th century congregations in their some-

All Saints, Croughton

In Croughton Church it is uncannily easy to lose one-self in the past, but the technological present is soon in evidence when one leaves it, for just outside the village is a well known US Air Force base.

Flight into Egypt, Croughton

what gruesome incident. The first of these subjects is especially well preserved. To increase enjoyment of the paintings the church thoughtfully displays a well illustrated book describing them in detail.

However, the attraction of Croughton Church lies not only in its pictures but also in a primitive beauty inside and out which gives them a perfect setting. There is evidence of Norman work in the fabric, the irregularities of which have a strange appeal. The squat tower with its undulating east wall, the non-alignment of clerestory and south aisle roofs and the non-vertical entrance to the south porch in no sense give the impression of dilapidation but rather suggest the loving and sensitive creation of an aged sculptor. Inside, the woodwork has an antique beauty: 15th century pews and chancel screen and Jacobean pulpit. The font is 13th century. On the north wall of the chancel there is a pedimented monument to John Clarke (died 1603) and his wife Jane. The east window by J. N. Comper depicts a company of saints with Christ in majesty above them.

KINGS SUTTON

THERE ARE CERTAIN architectural features the rail traveller looks out for: the tower of York Minster, the crooked spire of Chesterfield, the panorama of Oxford spires – and the spire of Kings Sutton church. From the train it creates a succession of pretty pictures, now rising high among houses and now glimpsed through trees, and at this distance it is recognised as a thing of beauty, as the jingle proclaims it. The spire is an inducement to visit the church, and after a drive along an open winding lane and a sharp turn through the village street there it is on the far side of the village green, with cottages on one side, Jacobean manor house among trees on the other side, and the village stocks in the foreground, presenting a more perfect picture than ever.

Here the beauty of the spire can be fully realised. To walk round it, noting the changing silhouette of clustered pinnacles and flying buttresses against the sky, and the rich variety of shapes in changing light is to agree that here is the most beautiful spire in a county that is famous for them. If the builder's aim saw elegance with lightness he succeeded brilliantly. From the cluster of ornate pinnacles, four rising from the battlements linked to a second four by delicate buttresses, the sparely crocketed spire shoots up to a height of 198 feet to create a 14th century masterpiece.

Hardly commanding the same instant admiration as the spire, the body of the church is nevertheless impressive, combining work of the 12th to the 16th centuries with fairly extensive restoration by Sir Gilbert Scott in the 19th. At the foot of the tower there is a beautiful west porch, Perpendicular and pinnacled, with a canopied niche over the entrance which once held a figure of Our

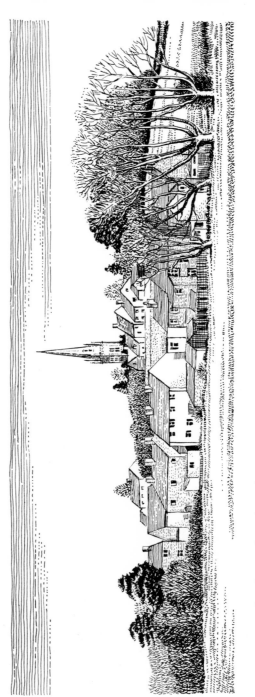

Kings Sutton Church seen from the railway

Lady, but admittance is usually through the south porch, which is also Perpendicular, though battlemented and with a groined roof.

Inside, the church is lofty, airy and spacious, the nave and aisles mostly Decorated, with some earlier work in the south aisle, while the unusually long chancel is largely Norman, as might be expected from the intact row of corbels on the outside walls. On each side of the chancel are six stone seats inset in blank arcading that retains the original Norman shafts but their semi-circular arches have acquired a zig-zag pattern during restoration. The organ is neatly recessed in the chancel's north wall. The handsome oak chancel screen of eight bays, with some fine tracery at the head, is to Scott's design, and his poppyhead stalls are grandly in keeping.

There is a noteworthy memorial to Thomas Langton Freke (died 1769) attributed to John Bacon, representing the Triumph of Christ over Death, in which the three figures of the victorious Saviour, the recumbent skeleton of Death, and a kneeling angel are expressively wrought. Looking west from the chancel, the contribution to the spaciousness of the building made by the generously wide aisles, the lofty 16th century clerestory and the great tower arch can be appreciated.

On leaving the church, as on entering it, one's attention is taken by the large Norman font. Six-sided, roughly hewn, and probably a travesty of what it once was, it is associated with the little-known St. Rumbold. According to legend, he was the son of the King of Northumbria, who lived only three days and apparently preached a sermon in that time, (but locally it is pointed out that the three days probably refer to his life after baptism)). He was baptized somewhere here and it is known that this is where he was baptized, in a font that was greatly reverenced during the Middle Ages. Perhaps the present font is part of it.

SS Peter and Paul, Kings Sutton

MIDDLETON CHENEY

'YOU HAVE COME to see the windows?' From long experience of showing people round, the rector assumed that this was the visitor's main interest. Yet his church has many beauties from centuries long before the Pre-Raphaelites created the splendid windows that are bringing more visitors to Middleton Cheney now that the work of the Brotherhood is again in fashion.

The tall Perpendicular spire rising about 150 feet from an eight-pinnacled tower is as much a landmark as the spires of Bloxham, Adderbury and Kings Sutton so that the rhyme could well be revised to include all four, and like the other three it pin-points an impressive building. Among the older houses of a village that has been expanded more than most by new housing developments, the church stands as a fine monument to 14th century building, or more precisely to a great church builder of that century, William of Edyngton, who became Bishop of Winchester. Formerly rector here, he built this church to replace one of the 12th century, and it may be his likeness that is preserved in one of the corbels.

On entering the south porch, attention is drawn to the steeply-pitched stonevaulted roof supported by three beams of interlocking stones. As the rector points out, this type of construction using no timber is found in the porch of only two other churches, of which the sister church of Chacombe is one, the other being at Corby. The porch and doors of the same age are an introduction to the 14th century Decorated work that claims attention in the spacious interior, notably the lofty nave arcades of four arches each, with clustered pillars and plain capitals. The aisle windows are also in Decorated style. The clerestory, added in the 15th century, is crowned by a fine painted ceiling, with which the painted pulpit and the graceful chancel screen are contemporary. All these date from 1460, owing their present richness to Sir Gilbert

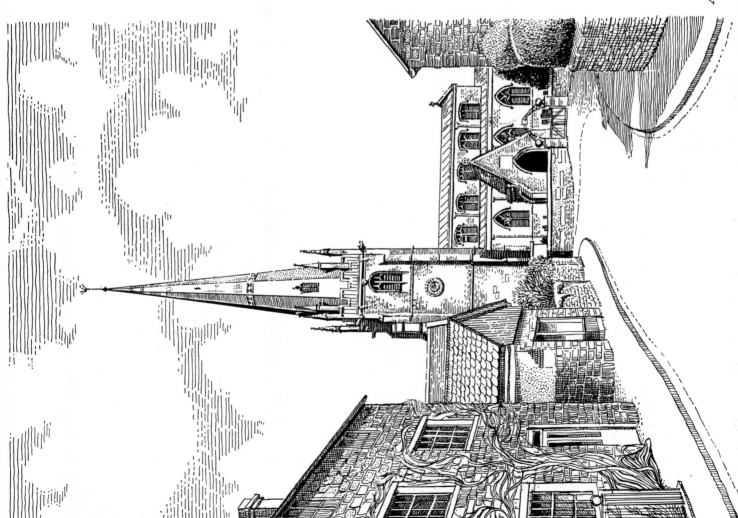

All Saints, Middleton Cheney

St. James, Newbottle

Scott who restored the church with fair restraint in 1865, when he added the canopy to the chancel screen.

Inevitably, one is attracted time and again by the windows. The reason why Middleton Cheney is so rich in Pre-Raphaelite glass from the William Morris work-shop, having eight such windows to Bloxham's one is that a former rector, Rev. W. E. Buckley (who is com-memorated in two of the chancel windows), was a personal friend of Sir Edward Burne-Jones.

The west window (tantalisingly high in the wall) includes the original of that artist's famous work, 'The Six Days of Creation', comprising six lights each with an angel holding a globe. But these are outshone by the three figures below them, Shadrach, Meshach and Abednego of the Book of Daniel, The Three Holy Children of the Apocrypha, who are seen praising their Creator as golden flames swirl round them. At the top of the window are Adam and Eve,

The glorious east window, enriched by delicate tracery, is inspired by the Epistle for All Saints Day. It provides not only a rich and colourful galaxy of the great from Scripture and the early Church, but also (like some of the other windows) a guessing game: Who was the artist responsible for each figure? Burne-Jones, William Morris, Ford Madox Brown, Simeon Solomon and Philip Webb are all involved, but authorities disagree about some of the attributions.

The east window of the north aisle is also a composite work, in which are depicted the Virgin, (Burne-Jones) SS Anne and Elizabeth (Brown) and the Annunciation (Morris), with coats of arms (probably Webb). Dante Gabriel Rosetti, perhaps the most talented of the Brother-hood, may have designed the window in this aisle show-ing Elijah, although some think it is by Morris. Samuel in the adjacent window is by Burne-Jones. In the chancel, the Buckley memorial windows are also by Burne-Jones, and opposite them are Old Testament themes by Brown and Webb. A little gem of a window by Webb above the chancel arch shows the Dove, representing the Holy Spirit.

It would be a pity if visitors were so enthusiastic about the windows that they failed to walk round to the west door. This is worth seeing, having a niche on each side in which stand figures of the Virgin and the Angel of the Annunciation, with a frieze of angels above them, Such visitors may also be unaware of the graves nearby of Roundheads who died at the Battle of Middleton in 1643.

NEWBOTTLE

FOR AN IDYLLIC Sunday afternoon in spring, with sunlight streaming through the trees, primroses and blue-bells in abundance and the birds singing, Newbottle is the choice of many Banbury families – Newbottle Woods, a peaceful place despite its popularity and occasional motor traffic.

Newbottle itself, now no more than a manor house, a church, a vicarage and a cottage, is just as attractive in its way and just as peaceful. It is a tree-enclosed cul-de-sac, once the centre of a village of which the houses were allowed to crumble centuries ago when its people moved to Charlton a mile away. Once the smaller of the two, Charlton continues to grow, but villagers still go to church in Newbottle as they have been doing since Norman times.

Few traces of the Church's Norman past remain, apart from the font, which is the simplest of tub shapes on a simple square plinth, but there is evidence of only slightly later work in the tower and in the rather crude piscina. The building in largely 14th century Decorated, with an Early English chancel. The nave arcades of four arches each are supported by octagonal pillars. The pulpit, inlaid with a simple pattern, was made in 1584, but the sturdy chancel screen, ornamented with carvings, may be the original of two centuries before.

There are several memorials in the church, the most prominent, dated 1655, being a monument by John Stone to John Cresswell and his wife who lived at Purston. Formerly set in an arch with carved drapery, their busts in white marble stand side by side beneath their coat of arms. A notice in the church porch draws attention to the brasses from which rubbings may be taken upon payment of a fee, which is now a common and reasonable requirement in view of the increasing popularity of brass-rubbing leading in time to the inevitable disfigurement of the brasses. The popularity of the brass in the chancel to Thomas Dormer (died 1555) and his family can be imagined, for he is portrayed with his two wives and their nineteen kneeling children. By comparison, Albert Pymm, the subject of an uncommon 19th century brass, appears in lone state. A more usual memorial of that century is the glass in the east window dated 1893, representing the Crucifixion, in memory of Lady Elizabeth Leslie-Melville-Cartwright.

There is no memorial in the church to the most famous man to live in the parish, F. E. Smith, Earl of Birkenhead, sometime Lord Chancellor. It is to be found in the grave-yard at Charlton where he is buried with other members of his family, including his elder daughter Lady Eleanor Smith, famous for her novels of gypsy life.

WARKWORTH

ONE IMAGINES THE congregation being unusually devout. Whether living in Warkworth or Overthorpe, worshippers have to walk some distance through open fields, which might well deter all but the most faithful, especially in winter, while those who do attend all the

St. Mary, Warkworth

year round have ample opportunity to consider the bounty of nature through the changing seasons. Moreover, despite extensive restoration during the second half of last century, the building seems to draw from the history reposing in it an atmosphere of devotion, perhaps intensified by its isolation.

However, the church was not always so isolated, with only a farm as neighbour. Nearby stood the mediaeval Warkworth Castle, home of the Lyons and Chetwode families, which was converted into a Jacobean mansion by the Holmans when they bought it in 1629. The house was demolished in 1806 and all that remains is a stone carved with the Lyons and Chetwode arms built into the farm wall. All three families are commemorated in the church, however, by memorials which alone are worth a pilgrimage through the fields.

On entering by the south door, the visitor is attracted immediately to the east end of the north aisle, where he sees one of the most remarkable altar tombs in Britain. Distinctively white, in contrast to the warm stone of the church interior, it is carved from hard chalk (or 'clunch') which has preserved intact the genius of some 14th century craftsman. This is the tomb of Sir John de Lyons (died 1350) whose recumbent effigy in battle order is carved in elaborate detail. Round the sides, in unusually high relief, are panels showing mourning figures, shields and square quatrefoils. At the foot, in a canopied niche, stand small figures of the Madonna and Child probably of the same date as the tomb but not part of it. In two arched recesses in the north aisle are effigies of this knight's parents, Sir John (died 1312) and Lady Margaret de Lyons.

While the Lyons monument is immediately eye-catching, the Chetwode memorials are to be found under protective covers. They are fine (if rather strangely proportioned) brasses mostly in excellent condition,

which were almost lost during the church's restoration in 1841. Strangely enough they were rejected by the architect but saved by the builder and were reinstated when the church was much more successfully restored in 1869. This explains why most have been relaid in cement.

Altogether, five brasses commemorate three generations: Sir John Chetwode (died 1412), now weirdly represented by the upper part of a body without head, set upside down in relation to the inscription; his wife Lady Amabella (Straunge) (died 1430) attractive in the dress of the period; their son and daughter John Chetwode and Margery Brownyng (both died 1420), the one in full armour standing on a lion and the other with a lap dog at her feet; and John's son-in-law, William Ludsthorpe (died 1454) in Milanese-type armour with a large decorated tilting helmet.

The Holman memorials are beautifully carved and well preserved 17th century marble gravestones in the floor of the nave before the chancel step.

The restoration in 1869 was made possible through the munificence of Mary Ann Horton of Middleton Cheney, founder of the alms houses there and of the Horton Infirmary in Banbury. She rebuilt the chancel, repaired

both aisles, provided an organ chamber and priest's vestry and gave a dignified pulpit and reading desk. The east window is in her memory.

Restoration left intact some fine carving on pew ends, including two exquisite pieces representing the Annunciation and a group of donors, and some carved inscriptions in Latin stripped on to the backs of pews. All these are from the 15th century, but the foliage and grotesque heads that decorate the capitals of the high nave arcades are two centuries older.

The shafts themselves, octagonal in Early English style, are heavily restored like much of the fabric. Some Decorated work of the 14th century is to be seen in the walls and windows and in the tower. The very unusual south transept, probably built as a chantry chapel in the 13th century, also has Decorated features, notably the piscina. The font is early Decorated, its large bowl carved with tracery that no doubt matched the windows of the period.

This is a church that makes demands on its congregation but surely rewards them. It imposes a discipline – and a seemly humility – on its preachers too, for they must stoop low to enter the pulpit.

Warkworth, Church across the fields